JEFF CORWIN
A WILD LIFE

THE AUTHORIZED BIOGRAPHY

PUFFIN BOOKS
An Imprint of Penguin Group (USA) Inc.

To Marina, Maya, and Natasha

With special thanks to Danielle Denega

PUFFIN BOOKS

Published by the Penguin Group

Penguin Young Readers Group, 345 Hudson Street, New York, New York 10014, U.S.A.

Penguin Group (Canada), 90 Eglinton Avenue East, Suite 700, Toronto, Ontario, Canada M4P 2Y3

(a division of Pearson Penguin Canada Inc.)

Penguin Books Ltd, 80 Strand, London WC2R 0RL, England

Penguin Ireland, 25 St Stephen's Green, Dublin 2, Ireland (a division of Penguin Books Ltd)

Penguin Group (Australia), 250 Camberwell Road, Camberwell, Victoria 3124, Australia

(a division of Pearson Australia Group Pty Ltd)

Penguin Books India Pvt Ltd, 11 Community Centre, Panchsheel Park, New Delhi - 110 017, India

Penguin Group (NZ), 67 Apollo Drive, Rosedale, North Shore 0632, New Zealand

(a division of Pearson New Zealand Ltd.)

Penguin Books (South Africa) (Pty) Ltd, 24 Sturdee Avenue, Rosebank, Johannesburg 2196, South Africa

Registered Offices: Penguin Books Ltd, 80 Strand, London WC2R 0RL, England

Published by Puffin Books, a division of Penguin Young Readers Group, 2009

1 3 5 7 9 10 8 6 4 2

THE LIBRARY OF CONGRESS HAS CATALOGED THE PUFFIN CHILDREN'S BOOK EDITION AS FOLLOWS:

Corwin, Jeff.

Jeff Corwin : a wild life : the authorized biography / Jeff Corwin.

p. cm.

ISBN 978-0-14-241403-3

[1. Corwin, Jeff—Juvenile literature. 2. Biologist—United States—Biography—Juvenile literature.
3. Herpetologists—United States—Biography—Juvenile literature.] I. Title.

QL31.C73A3 2009

590.92—dc22

{B} 2009008092

Puffin Books ISBN 978-0-14-241403-3

Printed in the United States of America

At home with animals

Jeff often found animals—like frogs, turtles, and snakes—while he was out exploring. So he brought these animals home with him to study and learn about them. He and his parents built cages and kept them for a short period of time. While he housed these animals, he learned a lot about biology from studying and observing. But Jeff's parents had a strict rule that after a few weeks, all critters must be released back to exactly the place where they were found. These animals belonged in the wild, and while it was okay for Jeff to watch them for a short time, they weren't pets.

Jeff's bedroom in Norwell quickly filled with aquariums, terrariums, and cages. Different types of snakes, lizards, reptiles, spiders, and bugs lived in each one. But his bedroom wasn't the only place these animals would occupy. Jeff would fill the toilet bowl with salamanders, scaring off guests who went to use the bathroom!

✩✩✩

READ ALL THE JEFF CORWIN BOOKS!

A note from Jeff corwin

Dear Reader,

   As far as I'm concerned, there's nothing more exciting than studying wildlife and exploring the natural world, and helping others to learn more about them. That's why I think I have the best job in the world. But I didn't always know what I wanted to do, and it wasn't always easy getting to where I am today.

   This biography will give you a peek at what my life was like growing up, and how I turned my love for animals into a fulfilling and rewarding career. I hope you enjoy reading it, and that you, too, will come to fully appreciate this wonderful world we live in.

Best wishes,

Jeff

CONTENTS

CHAPTER ONE

 **Snake Boy**

Have you ever had your teeth cleaned by a live shrimp? Jeff Corwin has, and that is just the beginning of the adventures he has had with animals. Jeff Corwin is one of the most celebrated wildlife biologists in the world, and his path there was paved with snakes. Yes, snakes! But let's not get ahead of ourselves.

Jeffrey Scott Corwin was born in Quincy, Massachusetts, on July 11, 1967. Quincy is an urban community located near the big city of Boston. Jeff lived in a three-family row house with his mom, Valerie, his father, Marcy, and his younger sister, Amy.

Jeff began learning about animals when he was just three years old. That was when he was given his first pet—a goat! Jeff's parents purchased the goat from a farm on Cape Cod. Jeff's mom named the goat Billy. The Corwin family thought Billy was a Nubian dwarf goat, which are good pets since they are small and weigh only about twenty to thirty pounds. But to everyone's surprise, Billy grew to be a hundred pounds! That's because he was actually a billy goat, which gets much larger than a Nubian dwarf goat.

Jeff loved Billy, and Billy was a part of the family. He even appears in family photos from Jeff's birthday parties. The Corwin family made a pen for Billy the billy goat on the lawn of their house in Quincy. Goats normally live on farms, so the sight of a goat living in the Corwins' front yard got a lot of attention from the neighbors! Jeff says that local people sometimes still mention Billy, saying, "You guys had that goat!"

Aside from Billy the goat, Jeff had few chances to experience animals in Quincy. Quincy is home to many tall buildings and paved streets, but little wildlife. Jeff had a hunger to explore the natural world and have adventures in it. But Quincy did not offer much opportunity for that. So Jeff had to make his own adventures.

When Jeff was a small child, he built a lean-to fort in the courtyard outside his house. He spent his time searching the neighborhood for wildlife. Jeff looked in the neighbors' yards and sheds for things like insects and abandoned nests. When he found something, he brought it back to his lean-to retreat. There, Jeff would examine, study, and display his findings. And he'd invite kids from the neighborhood over to have a peek, too. It was like he set up his own little museum!

Jeff's parents encouraged his interest in wildlife. Jeff's father, Marcy, loved nature. But he worked a lot, doing many different types of jobs. Marcy did everything from selling homes as a real estate agent to delivering doughnuts. He wanted to make sure there was always enough money with which to support his family. Eventually, Marcy Corwin got a well-paying, stable job as a Boston police officer.

After that, Marcy spent most of his time patrolling Boston's streets, keeping the city safe. But whenever he had the time, he would share his love of nature with Jeff. Marcy always loved birds and animals, and he was excited when Jeff took an interest in these things as well.

Whenever Marcy had time off from work and other responsibilities, he and Jeff would often head out to the country—to the Blue Hills Reservation area of Massachusetts. The Blue Hills Reservation is a seven-thousand-acre historical and natural area with many different types of animals, plants, and habitats, like forests, marshes, ponds, and meadows. There, father and son looked for local wildlife, like frogs and turtles. Sometimes Jeff and Marcy would take fishing trips. While Jeff loved to fish, he also searched for bugs and turtles on these trips. On other occasions, Jeff and his dad would simply head to a nearby pond at a golf course, where they looked for frogs.

Jeff's mom, Valerie, worked as a nurse when Jeff was growing up. She was also supportive of Jeff's love of nature. Valerie allowed him to watch animal-related television shows. When Jeff was a child, Animal Planet and other cable networks that now show nature programming were not around yet. So Jeff watched shows such as *Mutual of Omaha's Wild Kingdom*. He imagined being a part of these shows, exploring the natural history and life of animals.

As Jeff grew up, he loved animals more and more. That is why he treasured visits to the country to see his extended family. The Corwins often spent time at the home of Jeff's relatives in Holbrook, Massachusetts. Holbrook is a much more rural area than Quincy, so it offered Jeff lots of opportunities to explore nature. It was during one of these trips to Holbrook that Jeff had an important life experience—one that would change him forever.

At the age of six, Jeff was looking through a pile of wood in the yard of his relatives' house. At the bottom of the woodpile, Jeff spied a coiled-up mass with scales and a flickering tongue. It was a garter snake! Jeff had never seen a snake before. But it was love at first sight. Or, rather, love at first bite.

The creature slithered farther back into the woodpile, out of Jeff's sight. Jeff panicked. He worried that he might never see it again. So he frantically searched the woodpile for the snake, and was successful in finding it. But this time, Jeff didn't want to let the snake get away. So he reached down and grabbed the garter. And the snake grabbed Jeff right back. The snake was afraid, and it bit Jeff on the arm!

Jeff ran into the house to find the adults. But the garter snake had sunk its teeth into Jeff and was hanging from his arm! Jeff's parents and relatives were shocked and scared by the sight before them.

Jeff's father quickly unclenched the snake's jaws and pulled it off Jeff's arm. Jeff's relative yelled, "Get it out of the house!" But Jeff did not understand what all the fuss was about. He wondered why everyone seemed afraid of the creature. Jeff felt that he had just made an amazing discovery. He did not want the adults to free the snake outdoors. What if he never saw something like it again?

So Jeff told the adults not to release the garter snake. Everyone looked around, confused. Why would Jeff possibly want to keep a *snake*? Jeff replied, "I love it." Nonetheless, Jeff's father released the snake in the yard. It needed to go back to its proper home.

Ever since then, Jeff Corwin has been attached to snakes—though not so literally! After the garter snake bit him, Jeff became obsessed with snakes, turtles, frogs, and other reptiles and amphibians. They were all he wanted to read about. So his mom gave Jeff a book about reptiles so he could learn more.

Jeff soon wore the book thin from reading it again

and again. He even took it to bed with him! Jeff memorized the pages full of information and studied the photographs, dreaming of actually being in the swamps and seeing the animals up close for himself. He knew that for the rest of his life he wanted nothing more than to be around animals—to study them and experience them. His fascination with animals, particularly snakes, earned him the nickname Snake Boy.

Jeff says that the moment he discovered the garter snake in the woodpile was the moment he became a naturalist. He realized that he enjoyed studying the natural world, especially animals. Jeff often says that if he had pulled apart that woodpile and uncovered a golf club, he might have become Tiger Woods instead!

The Corwin family also spent a good deal of time visiting Jeff's grandparents in the town of Middleborough, Massachusetts. Middleborough is located even farther south than Holbrook. And just like Holbrook, Middleborough is a rural area. On these weekend trips to the country, Jeff enjoyed investigating the fields and meadows near his grandparents' home.

As he explored, Jeff made it his mission to find

another snake. And he did! One day at his grandparents' house, Jeff discovered another garter slithering around outside. This time, he didn't grab it. He was excited just to have found another creature like the one that had bitten him. From that day forward, every time Jeff visited his grandparents, he would find the same snake and simply watch it.

For two whole years, Jeff observed the snake's behaviors. He watched it eat, breed, and prey on other animals. He studied it, sketched it, and collected its molted (or shed) skins. By the time Jeff was eight years old, he had developed a strong bond with the garter snake.

But then, something awful happened. One day, Jeff sat alone in the yard, quietly observing his garter snake. Suddenly, the snake seemed to come apart right in front of him! Jeff was shocked and horrified to see his beloved garter snake writhing in pain. Its head had separated from the rest of its body, and its mouth was still reaching out and biting. Jeff's snake was dead in an instant.

Jeff looked around, confused and upset. He then looked up; over him stood a neighbor holding a garden spade. The neighbor had attacked the garter snake with the spade. He feared the snake would bite Jeff. The neighbor asked Jeff if he was all right. But Jeff was heartbroken and instead of answering, he quickly ran inside to his grandparents, thinking, No, I'm not all right!

Jeff had just witnessed the most horrible thing he could have imagined. He was shocked by the neighbor's reaction to the garter snake. He wondered why a person would kill a creature that wasn't harming anything. He knew that he needed to stop other people from needlessly harming animals out of ignorance and without a justifiable or legitimate reason. That was the day that Jeff Corwin became a conservationist.

Soon after the death of Jeff's favorite garter snake, the Corwin family moved. It was the summer of Jeff's eighth birthday. It was also the year that the Corwins welcomed their third child into the family—Jeff's youngest sister, Joy. The family of five chose to leave behind the urban bustle of Quincy. They moved to the country to a town called Norwell, Massachusetts. It was a move that suited Jeff's interests in animals and nature very well.

The night before the big move, Jeff lay awake, excited. His mind raced with thoughts of living somewhere that would allow him to have all the nature adventures he had ever dreamed of. He knew that, unlike Quincy, Norwell offered woods, marshes, and other places for discovery and exploration.

The day the family arrived in Norwell, Jeff immediately set off into the woods behind his new house. The woods became Jeff's classroom, where he worked on his skills as a naturalist. As he was exploring among the pine and oak trees, Jeff found an old, abandoned log cabin with a stone fireplace. The cabin stood next to a small pond and swamp. For the next ten years of his life, Jeff spent much of his time discovering and learning there. He loved all that his new hometown had to offer. He could finally experience all the wildlife he had been longing to see.

Jeff often found animals—like frogs, turtles, and snakes—while he was out exploring. So he brought these animals home with him to study and learn about them. He and his parents built cages and kept them for a short period of time. While he housed these animals, he learned a lot about biology from studying and observing. But Jeff's parents had a strict rule that after a few weeks, all critters must be released back to exactly the place where they were found.

These animals belonged in the wild, and while it was okay for Jeff to watch them for a short time, they weren't pets.

Jeff's bedroom in Norwell quickly filled with aquariums, terrariums, and cages. Different types of snakes, lizards, reptiles, spiders, and bugs lived in each one. But his bedroom wasn't the only place these animals would occupy. Jeff would fill the toilet bowl with salamanders, scaring off guests who went to use the bathroom. There was a falcon soaring across the porch, and a gigantic snapping turtle that Jeff had hauled home from a nearby pond. This turtle became a staple in the Corwin household. Jeff would catch and release the same turtle, year after year.

Jeff's mother became used to cleaning Jeff's room and getting up close and personal with his animals. Sometimes a snake would slither out from under a shirt or a squirrel would scamper across the room! There was also an ill-tempered iguana with an injured arm that Jeff's parents helped nurse to health. The Corwins gave the hurt iguana doses of antibiotics. When the iguana was finally healed, its personality changed. It became so much nicer than when it was hurt, they named it Fluffy!

Throughout the rest of his childhood in Norwell, Jeff's interest in and love for animals grew only stronger. Animals abounded, and the Corwins' house eventually became like a zoo. Little did Marcy and Valerie Corwin know, Jeff's experiences with animals had only just begun.

CHAPTER TWO

Once Bitten

For most kids, a snakebite would create a lifetime fear of the slithering creatures. But Jeff Corwin was no ordinary kid. Rather than fear snakes, Jeff decided to learn all he could about them, as well as other animals.

After moving to Norwell, in addition to exploring his wooded backyard, Jeff also spent time at one of the local wildlife centers. Beginning in junior high school, he volunteered at the New England Wildlife Center. The center provides care for sick, injured, and orphaned wild animals. Once the animals are well, they are released back into their natural habitat again.

The New England Wildlife Center was originally located in Hingham, Massachusetts. (The center is now located in Weymouth, Massachusetts.) Hingham is less than ten miles north of Norwell, where the Corwins now lived. Many days after school and on weekends, Jeff would ride his bike to the center. He busied himself caring for animals. He did things like fix broken bird wings and build fiberglass turtle shells for turtles that had been run over by cars. Jeff was learning about animals and helping them survive.

But Jeff couldn't get enough of animals! He also volunteered at the South Shore Natural Science Center, a museum located right in Norwell. It is a nonprofit organization that educates people about the natural environments of the south shore of Massachusetts. The center has several acres of conservation and recreation land, with meadows, woodlands, and a pond. Jeff spent many afternoons and weekends working there. He helped catalog their collection of animals and maintain their live critters. Jeff also taught classes about nature to other kids. But Jeff never forgot his love of snakes. And according to naturalist Barbara

Devine, Jeff always had a snake around his neck when he walked through the door.

Between the ages of ten and thirteen, Jeff also spent time visiting a traveling snake show in his area. The snake show was held at malls and county fairs, among other places. A local biologist named Fred Dodd was in charge of the snake show. Fred brought different types of snakes to display. Every time the snake show was in town, Jeff attended. Eventually, Jeff befriended Fred and was allowed to interact with some of Fred's snakes. Jeff also helped Fred by doing chores, such as cleaning cages. Fred even let Jeff take a snake home with him sometimes!

At that time, Fred was doing graduate study work in Belize. Belize is a country in Central America that is home to an ecosystem called the rain forest. Fred was in charge of an organization that took teams of researchers into the jungles of Belize to learn about the wildlife there. Jeff was very interested in hearing about these trips. And by the time he was thirteen, he was itching to go along. He wanted to see more snakes!

So Jeff asked his parents for permission to go on one of the weeklong trips to Belize. But Marcy and

Valerie Corwin felt that Jeff was too young to go on such a long trip without them. So they said no. But Jeff asked time and time again for their permission. Eventually, his parents agreed that when he was old enough, Jeff could go. But there was a catch: Jeff would have to pay his own way. Marcy Corwin told his son to come back and ask again in a few years when he had earned the money. Jeff took his father's words very seriously.

For the next three years, Jeff worked hard doing any job that would help him earn money to go to the rain forest. He bused tables at restaurants and even worked after hours cleaning and waxing the floor of a pub. After every hard day of work, Jeff thought, I'm a few dollars closer to getting there.

Finally, when Jeff was sixteen years old, he asked his parents about the rain forest again. But this time, the high school junior was holding a brown paper bag. It contained about fourteen hundred dollars! Jeff had saved every cent he earned.

Jeff had a simple request: he wanted a passport and his parents' permission to go to Belize with Fred Dodd. Marcy and Valerie Corwin were shocked, and very proud of their son's determination. They knew it was Jeff's dream. He had worked hard and earned the privilege of being allowed to go. So that summer, Jeff took a trip to Belize. And it was a trip that changed him forever.

During his time in Belize, Jeff stayed with a research team studying the amphibians, reptiles, and other wildlife of the rain forest. He saw and experienced many animals for the first time. He spent a night in a Mayan village in a thatch house with an earth floor, went exploring at night for snakes and frogs, and swam down a river with toucans and iguanas in the trees hanging over the water. He began to understand just how complicated the rain-forest ecosystem is. Jeff learned what it was like for the indigenous, or local, people living there to interact with nature so closely.

While on that trip, Jeff also had his first experience getting lost in the wilderness. Late one afternoon, Jeff went out exploring by himself. He headed deep into the rain forest, watching the trail in front of him the whole time. After a while, Jeff turned around to trace the path behind him. That was when he realized he was in big trouble!

When Jeff turned to study the path he would use to get back to camp, there appeared to be many different possible paths that he could have just taken. Darkness came quickly, and Jeff was completely lost! Thankfully, he had a headlamp on, so he was not completely in the dark. When Jeff did not return to camp, a whole team of people went out searching for him. But it was about four hours before he was rescued! Jeff learned a valuable lesson, however: when exploring in the woods, always trace the path in front of you *and* the one behind you in order to get back to where you started.

In the rain forest, Jeff felt more like himself than ever before. There was just so much to discover and learn! He knew he needed to go back there as often as possible. For the next ten years of his life, Jeff worked hard to keep paying for plane tickets to return to Belize. But by the time he was in college, he was getting paid to be there! Jeff was leading his *own* research expeditions to the rain forest.

Jeff's time in Belize made him feel so strongly about conserving the rain forest that he would later spend more than two years combined living and studying there. And because of all his experience and research, Jeff is now an expert in rain-forest animals. And today, he is still in touch with biologist Fred Dodd.

While Jeff had some unusual experiences during high school—not many teenagers travel to the jungle—he also had more typical experiences. Like most teenage boys, Jeff argued with his little sisters and got into some trouble with his parents.

When Jeff was seventeen years old, his parents had to go to a funeral. They gave Jeff permission to borrow their car while they were gone. He was to take his little sister Amy out for some ice cream. As Jeff was backing the car out of the driveway, he and Amy began to argue and tease each other. Amy pulled at Jeff's hair, and a full-out wrestling match started! But the quarreling siblings forgot one very important thing: the car was already moving.

When Jeff and Amy realized the car was rolling, Jeff panicked. He slammed his foot down on the pedal he thought was the brake. He intended to stop the car. But he accidentally hit the gas pedal, instead. This made the car go flying at a high rate of speed, crashing through a fence. Jeff was finally able to hit the brakes, but by that time, the car was hanging over the edge of the Corwins' swimming pool!

Amy teased Jeff, "You're in so much trouble! Mom and Dad are going to *kill* you!" But Jeff managed to drive the car out and park it in the driveway again. When Jeff's parents came home, they saw the damage to the car and the fence. Jeff was definitely in big trouble! (Even as an adult, Jeff has found himself in trouble driving—this time for getting too many speeding tickets. Some things never change!)

Jeff also had some trouble in school. Like many other kids, Jeff felt like he did not always fit in. Jeff was a little overweight, and sometimes he acted out as the class clown, joking around and entertaining his peers by doing voices and impersonations.

And his clowning around didn't help his grades. Jeff had a tough time in high school, partly because he was not a very good student. He actually failed high school biology! It's hard to believe that a famous biologist failed biology as a teenager, but it is true. Jeff did not succeed in a traditional school setting and thought maybe he just was not all that smart.

Luckily, Jeff discovered the drama department

at Norwell High School. He performed in musical theater productions and really enjoyed it. His favorite character was the evil Wazir of Baghdad from a musical called *Kismet*. Singing and acting gave Jeff a creative outlet for all the energy he used to spend entertaining the class!

Jeff says that his time spent performing onstage made high school much easier for him to deal with. His drama teacher, Mrs. Beal, saw that Jeff was a gifted actor and performer. And she encouraged him to keep at it. Jeff had found his calling, and, as they say, the rest is history! Jeff does television programs today because of his involvement in theater during high school.

Jeff graduated from Norwell High School in 1985. Even though he loved nature and theater, he was feeling lost and wasn't sure what to do with his life. That's when Jeff decided to join the Army National Guard. During the summer of 1985, Jeff spent about eight weeks at army boot camp at Fort Leonard Wood, in Missouri. Boot camp was very physically challenging. And with all the exercise, Jeff began to lose weight.

After boot camp, Jeff realized that if he was ever going to become a biologist, he would have to go to college. His poor grades from high school made it hard for him to be accepted. But he knew he had to do something with biology in his life. He loved the subject too much to give up. Jeff was admitted to a small private college, but after a semester, he realized he wasn't ready to focus on his studies. He decided to leave and go into the army again.

Jeff knew the army could also help him pay for college, so in March 1986, Jeff went to Fort Sam Houston, in San Antonio, Texas, where he did his professional training in the army.

Jeff studied to be a medic, which is an onsite medical expert. He found the army challenging, but in a good way. He spent ten to twelve hours per day in the classroom or in the field, practicing his skills firsthand. Jeff felt that he was learning to be disciplined, which was something he needed.

While at Fort Sam, Jeff's days off were precious. On those days, the trainees were allowed to leave the base. But unlike the other trainees, Jeff did not want to go see the sites in downtown San Antonio. Rather, he wanted to explore the Texas countryside to find its native creatures, especially its snakes!

At first, the other trainees thought Jeff was a little

weird for wanting to do this. But after each trip out exploring, Jeff would report back with all the amazing things he had seen. So it wasn't long before the other trainees were clamoring to join Jeff on his journeys.

On one of his expeditions, Jeff and some friends came across a diamondback rattlesnake. It was the first rattlesnake Jeff had ever seen, and he was enthralled by its rattling noises. The other trainees were fearful of the rattlesnake and wanted to kill it. But the naturalist in Jeff prevented them from harming the serpent, and instead took that moment to give them a lesson on not destroying nature's creatures.

One day, while Jeff was still studying to be an army medic, he and some friends traveled to Corpus Christi on a day off. There they attended a rattlesnake roundup. A rattlesnake roundup is sort of like a carnival of snakes. People come from far and wide with thousands of snakes. Then they perform shows and exhibitions with the snakes. Jeff watched in horror as he witnessed people skinning rattlesnakes, frying up rattlesnakes for dinner, and cutting off a rattlesnake head to make a paperweight.

But that wasn't even the worst of it! Jeff also learned how so many people were able to find and capture so many snakes, and he wasn't happy about it. Snakes naturally live in the ground or in other deep, dark places, like rock walls. To get the rattlesnakes to come out of hiding, some people would spray gasoline into areas where they knew snakes might live. To escape the poisonous gasoline, rattlesnakes would emerge from their dens, only to be caught. But many of the rattlesnakes didn't make it that far. The gasoline often killed the rattlesnakes, as well as any other living creatures around them.

Jeff couldn't believe his ears, and he knew he had to do something—anything—to help the poor rattlesnakes. So he and his friends pooled their money and bought as many rattlesnakes as they could afford from vendors at the snake roundup. Then they released the rattlers back in to the Texas wilderness, where they belonged. Thankfully, snake roundups are illegal in most states today because of their cruel practices.

In May 1986, Jeff left Fort Sam as a certified advanced field medical specialist! He now had a set of skills he would find use for often. For example, Jeff was recently on an airplane when another passenger suffered a heart attack. Jeff was able to use his medic training to help the passenger!

Shortly after finishing his army training, Jeff applied to and was accepted to Bridgewater State College. But his acceptance had a condition: Jeff had to improve his academic skills significantly in order to stay. And with his newfound determination, he did just that. He took difficult courses, like anatomy, ecology, and anthropology, and got A's! Top students surrounded him: those preparing to be doctors, engineers, and biophysics experts. But among the best students, Jeff rose to the head of the class in the animal, anthropological, and ecological sciences.

Jeff recalls being in a very competitive anatomy class at Bridgewater State. One day, Jeff's professor challenged the class to identify a part of an animal they had not yet studied. The class was stumped—except for Jeff! He used his knowledge of animals and their biology to make an educated guess: he identified the part as the ossicle (a bony structure found inside the ear) of a whale. Jeff's professor was shocked—Jeff was correct! He told Jeff that in the twenty years he'd been asking students the same question, not a single student had been able to provide the correct answer.

While at Bridgewater State College, Jeff focused

his studies in not one, but two different areas—biology and anthropology. *But what about the snakes? you must be wondering.* Well, Jeff is a biologist who studies many animals, but he specializes in an area of biology called herpetology. Herpetology is the study of reptiles and amphibians, including snakes!

It took Jeff about seven years to complete his studies at Bridgewater State College. And they were a very busy seven years for him. He had to work in order to pay his tuition, so he got a job at Plimoth Plantation. Plimoth Plantation is a living historical museum located in Plymouth, Massachusetts. The people who work there dress in clothing appropriate for the time period. They also take on the role of a person living there in 1627. Jeff was living in Plymouth at the time, and the job was a great fit for his interests. He was fascinated by American history, and he got to be an actor again. His role: to play a seventeenth-century sailor aboard the *Mayflower*!

But science was never far from Jeff's heart. He also sought to protect the threatened rain forests of Central and South America. After spending so much time in Belize, it was a cause that had become very important to him. He wanted to do his part to help preserve this amazing ecosystem. Jeff says, "We need to look at how we reproduce, how we use our resources, and how we function as a global community. We are not far from the day when the only rain forests left are rain forests that are locked up in exclusive, restricted, private, and public sanctuaries." So with the help and funding of Bridgewater State College and a professor there named Dr. Jahoda, Jeff established the Emerald Canopy Rainforest Foundation. At this time, Jeff was only in his second year of college, but he was already starting his own nonprofit organization!

The Emerald Canopy Rainforest Foundation was an organization that helped to protect rain forests. The foundation taught people about the importance of protecting this fragile ecosystem. Humans are destroying rain forests, tearing them down and killing their plants and animals. And now there are many species of plants and animals there that are nearly extinct. And soon, there might be none left.

The highlight of Jeff's work with Emerald Canopy was when he served as a member of a youth action committee for the United Nations Environmental

Program (UNEP). The UNEP looks at the global environment and brings problems to the attention of governments and the international community. Jeff became involved with the UNEP during his third year at Bridgewater State. In 1993, just after his graduation, Jeff addressed an environmental conference at the General Assembly of the United Nations, which is a group of world leaders, conservationists, and other students. Jeff, as well as other students from around the word, spoke about environmental issues. Jeff's focus was on saving the rain forests.

But Jeff's work did not stop there. In his efforts to save the rain forests, Jeff took dozens of trips to Central and South America during college. While he was doing research and studying the environment, Jeff managed to have some crazy experiences, just as he does on his television shows today.

On one trip, he traveled to Belize to do his usual exploring of and learning about the rain-forest ecosystem. Late one night, he went for a hike by himself. That's when he spotted a pair of pygmy anteaters. Anteaters are animals found in Mexico, Central America, and South America. The pygmy anteater is the smallest species of anteater. They are covered with silky, golden-brown fur and have jaws that curve to form a short tube. Like their name tells us, pygmy anteaters eat ants and other insects.

Jeff had never seen a pygmy anteater before! The adorable animals weighed only about a half pound each and were tucked beneath a palm frond. Jeff decided he wanted to photograph the cuddly creatures. So he wrapped them in cloth and snuggled them to him. That's when one of them stuck its paw up Jeff's nose! It dug its claw into the skin of his sinus cavity. Jeff howled in pain. He tried to remove the anteater's claw, but that only seemed to make things worse. So Jeff had to wait until the anteater removed its claw on its own.

Jeff returned to his camp with a bloody nose. It looked as though he'd been in a fight. But his attacker was a tiny, gentle, fuzzy animal! Nonetheless, Jeff had two pygmy anteaters to show for it. He placed his precious, though feisty, friends safely in a box for the night. He intended to photograph the pygmy anteaters in the morning and then return them to their home.

That night, a local Mayan man explained to Jeff that there are stories of how pygmy anteaters have a strange ability to disappear. They escape from enclosed places, and nobody knows how they do it. The next morning, Jeff went to retrieve the anteaters from their box. But they were gone. Yet the lid of the box was still tightly closed! Just as the Mayan man explained to Jeff, the anteaters had somehow escaped from their box. It was as though they had never been there at all! And Jeff still doesn't know how they escaped!

On another trip shortly after that, when Jeff was twenty years old, he was traveling down the Aguarico River in the country of Ecuador in South America. A Cofán family was leading him. The Cofán people are native to certain parts of Ecuador and Colombia. The group was traveling in a dugout canoe. They were on their way to a faraway lake in the heart of the rain forest.

While drifting down the river one day, Jeff saw a thick vine draped over a tree limb. It was hanging down just a few feet above the water's surface. As the boat got closer, Jeff realized that it was no vine he was seeing. It was an anaconda!

Anacondas are large aquatic snakes that live in swamps and rivers in the rain forests of South America. Anacondas are members of the boa constrictor family. Like other types of boas, anacondas are not poisonous. They kill their prey by coiling their large, powerful bodies around their victims. Then they squeeze really hard. The anaconda's prey either suffocates or is crushed to death. The anaconda then unhinges its jaw and swallows the victim whole. Anacondas have been known to dine on caimans, which are relatives of the alligator, other snakes, deer, and jaguars.

Even though the snake was enormous, Jeff's first thought was that they should paddle the boat over to it so he could capture it! The native Cofán family thought Jeff was crazy, of course. But they agreed to let him try to get the anaconda on one condition: if anything went wrong, he was on his own!

Jeff positioned the canoe under the hanging snake. He was ready to try to pull it into the boat. But at the same moment, the snake began sliding off the tree branch and into the water. Its giant body was quickly disappearing beneath the surface! Jeff couldn't let the snake disappear. Just as he had done with the garter snake as a child in Massachusetts, Jeff reached out and grabbed the anaconda!

The snake didn't care for Jeff's movement toward

it. It began to thrash wildly under the water. But Jeff held on tight. He began pulling the snake into the boat foot by foot. At one point, its head swung around toward the front of the canoe. The passengers there screamed and quickly moved toward the back.

The snake dipped its head back into the river. Jeff continued pulling at it. He had most of the snake inside the boat. But Jeff needed to secure the creature's head in order to control it, and that was the only part still beneath the water.

Jeff nervously put his hand under the water and reached for the snake's neck. He knew that if he reached incorrectly, his hand would end up inside the giant mouth of the snake. Thankfully, Jeff made a lucky grab. He was able to hold the snake tightly near the top of its head. He heaved once more, and finally, the entire snake was in the canoe. Jeff quickly observed the snake and snapped a few photos. Then he slid the snake back into the water, where it belonged. Everyone else was very relieved when the anaconda was off the boat!

The summer that Jeff turned twenty-one, he visited the country of Greece on vacation. Jeff was out touring the city of Athens one day when he came upon a man with a snake. The man was telling pass-ersby all about the creature in his arms. Of course, Jeff saw the snake, and he immediately stopped to get a closer look!

Jeff talked with the man, whose name was Hercu-les Karalis. Jeff and Hercules shared a love of snakes and hit it off immediately. Before Jeff continued on his way, Hercules asked Jeff if he would be interested in returning to Greece the following summer. He wanted Jeff to come back and work with him at his serpentarium, or snake museum. Jeff enthusiastically agreed!

The following summer, when Jeff was twenty-two, he traveled back to Greece to work at Hercules' serpentarium in Athens. Hercules had built the snake museum in order to teach Greek people about their native reptiles. Jeff really enjoyed working with Her-cules that summer. Jeff lived with Hercules and his family in their home, so he got to know him very well. In fact, Jeff calls Hercules the Greek version of him!

When not working hard at the serpentarium, Jeff took advantage of his free time to travel around Greece, and other nearby countries, like Turkey and

Egypt. He observed wildlife in the area—especially its snakes!—and learned about archaeology, anthropology, and the local cultures.

One day, while riding a burro, or donkey, through the Valley of Delphi in Egypt, Jeff came across a sinkhole. A sinkhole is a hollowed-out area of stone that is connected to an underground cavern or passageway. He got off his mule to check it out, and what he found inside was incredible.

When Jeff shined his flashlight into the depths of the sinkhole, he found himself face-to-face with an ancient tomb filled with an entire family of mummies! A mummy is a dead body that has been preserved and wrapped up before burial. This was a very common practice in ancient Egypt. Jeff had seen mummies in photos and museums, but he'd never been quite so up close and personal with one before! He found it amazing to examine the details of these preserved pieces of history without glass or velvet ropes blocking his view. He was thrilled at the feeling that he had discovered something that perhaps nobody else had seen in thousands of years! Afterward, Jeff exited the sinkhole, respectfully leaving the mummies just as he'd found them.

Jeff's trips throughout the world, including to the rain forests of Belize, were always filled with interesting encounters with animals. And by the time Jeff graduated from college in 1992, he had had many adventures and successes. He had been in the military, had received two bachelor of science degrees—one in biology and one in anthropology—had started a foundation, and had numerous incredible animal adventures. But this was only the beginning for Jeff. The best was yet to come!

CHAPTER THREE

Almost Famous

After graduating from Bridgewater State College, Jeff returned to his beloved rain forests. He lived in Central America for most of the next few years and worked at a field station. A field station is a facility set up in an area that scientists want to study. By being in the middle of the area of interest, scientists are able to observe and document things more easily. So Jeff was in the middle of the rain forest, able to study everything! At that point in his life, Jeff figured his career path would be in academics. But then in 1994, Jeff got a taste for television.

Jeff's first big break in television was thanks to a man named Dr. Robert (Bob) Ballard. Dr. Ballard is an oceanographer, which means he is a scientist who deals with the oceans, including the water, the wildlife, and the health of these bodies of water. He discovered the shipwreck of RMS *Titanic*.

In 1994, Dr. Ballard was producing an educational documentary and interactive project series in association with National Geographic called the JASON Project. The JASON Project was a program that taught kids biology, the importance of wildlife, and the delicate balance of the environment and ecosystems. The JASON Project got its name from a Greek hero named Jason, who was an explorer. Dr. Ballard gave the organization its name because he wanted to spark students' imaginations with exploration and real-life science.

Jeff had met Dr. Ballard about a year prior at a reception at Bridgewater State College. At that time, Jeff pitched Dr. Ballard the idea of filming a segment of the JASON Project in the rain forests of Belize. Dr. Ballard thought it was an interesting idea and agreed to do it. He hired Jeff to be an expedition naturalist during their broadcast from Belize.

In 1994, Jeff spent two weeks doing live broadcasts from Belize. He did five live broadcasts per day and loved every moment of it. It was a welcome experience for him. He was able to serve as a naturalist, do hands-on fieldwork, and further expand his knowledge of wildlife. But perhaps best of all, Jeff was able to use his performing talents to share his passion for the rain forests with the world. It all felt very right to Jeff. He began to picture a career for himself that would allow him do more of the same.

After doing the broadcasts for Dr. Ballard, Jeff decided he wanted to turn his adventures in the wild into a television program that would both educate and entertain an audience. The friends and colleagues he met on the JASON Project encouraged Jeff to pursue this goal. So with their help, Jeff made trailer videos and sent them to various production companies. On these videos, Jeff talked excitedly about animals and his passion for conservation.

For the next two years, Jeff received many negative reactions to his television show ideas from industry insiders. People told him that he was simply not cut out for television, and that his ideas would not be popular with audiences.

By 1996, Jeff was feeling as though he should pursue other career paths. He decided to go back to school and enrolled in a graduate program at the University of Massachusetts at Amherst. Jeff continued his studies there until 2003, when he earned a master of science degree in wildlife and fisheries conservation. Not too shabby for a guy who failed high school biology!

Also in 1996, Jeff's personal life underwent a big change. That was the year he met his wife, Natasha. Natasha Soultanova is Russian, but was born and raised in Germany. One day, while grocery shopping in Harvard Square in Cambridge, Massachusetts, the couple met. Jeff knew he had found a very special woman, and they married only three months later.

Jeff had just enrolled in graduate school, and Natasha was still finishing her undergraduate studies at Brandeis University in Waltham, Massachusetts. This posed a problem for the young couple: they could not afford to pay for both educations. So Natasha put her studies on hold for a while so they could afford to pay for Jeff's schooling.

Jeff and Natasha were excited to be starting a new life together, but it was difficult for them. They packed up their belongings and moved to Deerfield, Massachusetts, where they lived for a year. They needed to be closer to Jeff's school. They had no car, little money, and no friends in their new town. But they had interesting experiences of their own—especially with their new apartment.

Their first apartment was in an old bakery located between a pickle factory and a candle factory. This was not a typical place to live. Jeff says, "There were always strange smells in our apartment!" Some days, their place smelled like vinegar from the pickle factory. Other days, it smelled overly sweet from the scented candles at the candle factory.

But just as they started their life together, that summer, Jeff returned to Belize by himself as a part of his graduate work. Jeff had been to Belize dozens of times, but this trip became his most memorable. He had a lot of responsibility there. He was researching bats and running a field station. Jeff was also conducting an inventory of amphibians and reptiles of the area. In doing that inventory, Jeff frequently came across a type of snake called a coral snake. And he discovered that there were many varieties living in Belize.

Coral snakes are generally small and brightly colored. They are part of the same very venomous family of snakes that includes the cobra. There are about fifty species of known coral snake, and most of them live in Central and South America. Coral snakes usually have a pattern of black, yellow, and red bands on them.

Shortly before Jeff was scheduled to leave the country to head home, he went out for one last hike. Jeff knew the area well and was comfortable hiking alone there. During the hike, Jeff encountered a coral snake.

Jeff wanted to stop the snake in order to observe it, so he tried to pin the snake gently with his walking stick. But before he could do so, it slithered away from him. Jeff did not want the snake to escape before he could examine it. So without thinking, Jeff pinned the snake down with his foot.

There were two problems with this situation: coral snakes have short fangs through which they inject poisonous venom. Their venom is deadly to humans. The other problem was that although coral snakes aren't usually mean, they will bite if bothered or held down.

And that is exactly what the coral snake did when

Jeff stepped on it. It bit Jeff's big toe, which was exposed in his sandals. Immediately, Jeff felt a terrible pain shoot up his foot into his leg. There he was, alone in the jungle, suffering, with a snakebite that could kill him within four hours.

Jeff had to think fast. He knew he needed antivenin. Antivenin is a cure for a snakebite, and Jeff needed to be given this antivenin in order to survive the bite. Jeff had been staying in the nearest village, so he knew its layout. He felt he had two possible options: He could try to hike to the local hospital. But the hospital might not have the antivenin he needed to survive. Jeff's second option was to hike to the site where he knew a small British international school was being constructed. Both places were miles away, so Jeff would have a long haul to get to either location.

This was a dangerous situation. The clock was ticking, so Jeff chose to make the long hike toward the British school site. He felt they might have the resources to get him out of the jungle and to a hospital that *did* have antivenin. As Jeff hiked, the pain in his leg got worse and worse. The snake venom spread quickly through Jeff's body.

Coral snake venom hurts the human nervous system, so Jeff's heart raced, he drooled, and his eyes watered. Jeff began to lose use of the leg that had been bitten, so he had to drag himself along.

One hour after being bitten by the coral snake, Jeff finally reached the British international school, where he was met with help. The staff there was able to contact the British embassy on Jeff's behalf. A British Defense Force helicopter was sent to get Jeff.

And that's when Valerie Corwin got a frightening phone call. The embassy called the Corwins to let them know what had happened to Jeff. They told Valerie and Marcy that someone was on their way to try to help Jeff, but that they might not make it in time to save his life.

When the helicopter arrived, it airlifted Jeff out of the jungle. It headed to a hospital, where he could receive antivenin. All the while, Jeff was calculating how much time he had left. He realized that the soonest he could possibly receive medical attention was three and a half hours after being bitten. By the four-hour mark, he could be dead.

Surprisingly, Jeff never really thought he would die. He did, however, realize what a foolish mistake he had made in getting too close to a coral snake. Fortunately, Jeff received the coral snake antivenin in time, and he was soon on his way to recovery.

But then Jeff had to face another frightening creature: his new wife. When it was clear that Jeff would be all right, Natasha was relieved but also very angry with Jeff. She was mad that he would act so carelessly. She reminded Jeff that he didn't belong only to himself anymore. He had a wife who loved and needed him.

After the snakebite scare, Jeff returned to his normal life back at home. He continued his graduate work, and he was earning money by waiting tables, tending bar, and doing voiceover work. Voiceover is when a person who cannot be seen speaks during a television show or movie. Since Jeff had always been talented at doing impressions and accents, it was a natural fit for him. He worked with a production company creating education videos for young people. He also played the lead role in a film called *Jaguar Trax*, in which Jeff portrayed a science teacher.

In 1997, Jeff and Natasha moved back to Cambridge, which was a place they knew and loved. Jeff commuted to Amherst a few times a week, which was "quite a hike," he says. It had been several years since Jeff had had his first taste of television with the JASON Project. Jeff had pretty much given up on the idea of being a television naturalist. But something inside him told him to keep trying. So he continued to meet with production companies, asking them to let him make a show.

Then one day, Jeff received the call he had been hoping for. Jeff heard from a production company called Popular Arts Entertainment that had seen his promotional videos. And they had good news: they sent Jeff's videos to Disney, and Disney was interested! An executive at the Disney Channel was impressed with Jeff's knowledge and relaxed personality. He thought Jeff would be great for television.

After meeting the people at the Disney Channel, Jeff was hired to create and host a nature show. So Jeff and a television crew traveled to Belize to film a pilot, or first episode, of *Going Wild with Jeff Corwin*. The pilot was well received by viewers, and the show was a go! Jeff was so enthusiastic about the opportunity that he decided to put his graduate study work on hold. Jeff's professors were surprised at the news of Jeff's television offer. In an interview with *UMass*

Magazine Online, one of his advisers, Curtice Griffin, said, "We were all shocked. We had no idea that those were his ambitions. We knew Jeff was a very energetic guy, always very creative, always making things happen. When he told us this was his dream and he had been offered the chance to do it, we told him, 'You'd be crazy not to.'"

From 1997 to 1999, Jeff cocreated, produced, and hosted the Disney Channel's *Going Wild with Jeff Corwin*. The program appealed to a family audience. It was equal parts fun and education. Jeff wanted to deliver his lessons with adventure and humor, and that he did. His fun behavior and animal knowledge made the show a hit. Jeff was thrilled with his new job. His dream had finally been realized.

The popularity of the show gave Jeff the chance to do a lot of cool things. Almost overnight, Jeff was a television star! People began to recognize him when he went out. Once, so many screaming fans greeted Jeff at an event, he required a police escort to get inside. And famous people loved Jeff, too!

While Jeff enjoyed his fame, he says that it was difficult trying to film animals for the show. Often-times, the best moments happened off camera. He once said, "I always think I should name my show *You Should Have Been Here Yesterday!*"

Going Wild with Jeff Corwin offered Jeff many chances to have more incredible adventures with wildlife. Once, the crew was filming the What's On the Menu portion of the show in Arizona. It was a brief segment that discussed how people in an area would interact with their natural sources of food. Jeff was trying to understand how the Native Americans there would have used the resources available to them, like bugs! Bugs are a source of food for many native peoples in the world. So Jeff was curious to try some out for himself.

He came across an old Native American recipe that included using harvester ants to create a gruel, a type of thin, watery porridge. Harvester ants live in dry or semidry parts of the world. They have a painful sting. To make sure they always have food, harvester ants harvest! They collect seeds and store them in special underground chambers for use when food is scarce.

When Jeff decided to make a meal from the harvester ants, he ignored one important detail—the recipe itself! Rather than cooking the critters, Jeff decided just to munch on some live ones! Now, as crazy as it sounds, Jeff had a logical reason for doing this. He had seen Africans eat live termites, and had done so himself in the past. So Jeff figured eating live ants would not be much different. That was, until he tried it!

Jeff chewed and chewed on the ants, but they would not die! The entire time, the ants were attacking the inside of Jeff's mouth. They injected acid into his cheeks, gums, and tongue as they bit. Jeff compared the feeling to chewing on glass and battery acid. For several weeks afterward, even though he brushed and scrubbed his teeth, he pulled bits of dead ant from his teeth, gums, and even from behind his tonsils!

Another time, Jeff was in Africa filming an episode of *Going Wild with Jeff Corwin*. He and his crew came upon a bull elephant. As he was working, Jeff watched the animal's ears closely. He knew that if his ears were flat against his head, he might charge at them. Jeff reminded his crew that if the elephant did charge, nobody should run away from it. Elephants chase after things that are running.

Jeff quietly watched the elephant. Then, all of a sudden, the elephant charged! But Jeff couldn't figure out why—he'd been so still. That was until Jeff turned around and saw his entire crew running away! Jeff's crew jumped in their vehicle and drove off. They had abandoned him!

Jeff found himself alone with a very angry elephant. He quickly walked into the woods and hid behind a tree. At that point, Jeff's crew drove back to the site. They saw Jeff's hiding spot, but they also saw that the elephant was on to him!

The elephant approached the tree and stuck its trunk around toward Jeff. From the truck, Jeff's crew calmly warned Jeff not to move. The elephant gave Jeff a good sniff, and must have decided he smelled good because he started pushing down the tree!

So Jeff moved to the next tree and hid again. Then he walked to the next tree and hid once more. The elephant finally grew bored with Jeff—he was too difficult to catch! Jeff eventually made his way back to the safety of the truck.

When Jeff was finally out of harm's way, his crew apologized for abandoning him. But they said they must have gotten a lot of great footage! However, when the footage of the elephant charge was viewed, it turned out to be nothing more than shots of the ground as the cameraman was running away! Everyone laughed about it in the end.

Jeff's Disney show was filled with adventures and was a wild success. It ran for more than four years. But sadly, in 1999, *Going Wild with Jeff Corwin* came to an end. Jeff was upset; he felt his dream job had been taken away too quickly. Jeff worried that perhaps he would never experience television success again.

The same year, Jeff's alma mater, Bridgewater State College, paid him a special honor, awarding him with a doctorate degree, or Ph.D., in education. They wanted to recognize Jeff for all his hard work in teaching others about caring for the environment and protecting endangered animals.

Although his television show ended, with all of his new experiences, Jeff kept very busy. He decided to resume his graduate work at the University of Massachusetts, and also began doing speaking engagements to earn money. Because he was a famous TV biologist, students and other animal enthusiasts wanted to listen to Jeff speak.

Through it all, Jeff reminded himself that although his television debut was a success, he didn't want to stop there. He was determined to move on to the next step in television. It was his own determination that had gotten him a successful television show. And with his passion for nature and his love of performing, he knew he could, and would, do it again.

CHAPTER FOUR

Creatures
Great and
Small

By 2000, Jeff's television career was thriving again. That year, the Discovery Network executives heard that TV personality Jeff Corwin was a free agent, and they quickly got in touch with him. Jeff was thrilled. The next thing he knew, he became the host and executive producer of his next television nature show, *The Jeff Corwin Experience.*

Jeff continued his graduate studies, finishing up his scientific research when he had time between filming. *The Jeff Corwin Experience* debuted in 2001. It aired in many countries to millions of viewers. Each week, Jeff takes his audience on a different journey to show them the varied wildlife on Earth, including snakes, crocodilians, primates, and eagles.

Jeff wanted *The Jeff Corwin Experience* to be informative, but also a whole lot of fun! Jeff feels that humor allows people to let down their guard and enjoy the learning process. He included funny fantasy segments in many episodes. And while he presents interesting facts, there are a few gross-out moments, too—like when he developed an interest in poop!

Feces, scat, waste, excrement—whatever you call it, Jeff has examined the poop of all creatures great and small. Jeff says that poop is a valuable biological learning tool. It not only tells you what animal is in the area, but also what it ate, how long ago it was there, how healthy it is, and even how big it is. Lots of information about an animal's history can be gathered from poop! Jeff says, "People can pooh-pooh poop, but there is science behind it. You may never see a tiger in India, but a steaming pile of poop will tell you it was there!"

And poop did just that on one particular trip to India. Jeff and his crew were there to try to film tigers.

The heat was an oppressive 108 degrees Fahrenheit, and they were all exhausted after days of searching. But when Jeff stumbled upon a fresh mound of tiger poop one day, he knew the creature wasn't far away!

The crew soon uncovered a stunning female tiger. As Jeff silently watched the tiger from a distance, he realized the tiger was watching something else—very, *very* closely. Jeff looked around and saw a small sambar deer drinking from a nearby water hole. That deer was looking mighty tasty to the tiger. The tiger crouched low, and Jeff waited in anticipation.

Suddenly, the tiger exploded toward the deer, swiping its massive paw at it. But the sambar proved too quick for the tiger. The deer leaped away from the tiger and scaled a steep slope to safety. Jeff says the experience reminded him that "for every successful hunt, there is an unsuccessful one." Nature is fair that way!

Like his other television shows, Jeff had lots of adventures while filming. Jeff often recalls filming an episode of *The Jeff Corwin Experience* in Namibia, a country in Africa. While on site, a cheetah popped up in the grass. Cheetahs are large cats and one of the fastest land animals in the world. These amazing

Jeff holding a coral snake, shot on location in Arizona for
The Jeff Corwin Experience.

White-Handed Gibbon

Jeff with a crocodile, taken during the filming of *Corwin's Quest*.

Jeff holding a reindeer calf, shot in Alaska for *The Jeff Corwin Experience*.

Burrowing Owl

Sitatunga

Shot on location in India for *The Jeff Corwin Experience*.

Jeff sleeping against a rhino.

Mongolian Bactrian Camel

Shot on location in Montana for *Corwin's Quest*.

Masai Giraffe

Squirrel Monkey

Jeff with a moose in Anchorage, Alaska, taken during the filming of *Into Alaska with Jeff Corwin*.

Black
Leopard

Baby Lynx

Shot on location in India for *The Jeff Corwin Experience.*

American
Bald Eagle

Jeff with a bear, taken during the filming of *Corwin's Quest*.

Black Bear

Tapir

Jeff Corwin with an orangutan.

mammals can accelerate to a running speed of more than sixty miles per hour in just a few seconds! Plus, they can sustain that speed for up to a thousand feet. Cheetahs used to be commonly found in open areas throughout Africa, the Middle East, and southwest Asia. But in the past one hundred years, unnecessary hunting and habitat destruction have reduced the cheetah's range and population.

The big cat was only about fifteen or twenty feet from Jeff and his producer. It started walking toward them, and Jeff's producer warned, "You can't outrun that cheetah." Jeff cheekily said, "I don't have to. I only have to outrun you." Jeff never really thought the cheetah would attack, of course. It was just another example of his using humor to lighten the mood.

The Jeff Corwin Experience also brought Jeff to the country (and continent) of Australia. There, Jeff came across one of Australia's ambassadors—the koala. He observed how koalas are being harmed by the encroachment of humans on their habitats. For example, there is one area in which a road cuts straight through a koala habitat, and koalas are being run over by cars.

Jeff is always saddened by examples like this. But

he was also encouraged by the innovative solution Australian conservationists found for this problem: koala tunnels! Koala tunnels have been built below roadways as a safe pathway through which koalas can pass to the other side of their habitat. In order to push the creatures to the tunnels, fences were constructed along the shoulder of the road. These fences have floppy tops, rather than rigid ones. The floppy tops make it nearly impossible for a koala to scale and climb over the fence, where it would then be in the road.

Instead, when the koala reaches the top of the fence, the fence flops over into the habitat, so the koala simply falls to the ground again. Then the koala walks along the base of fence, looking for an opening. That's when it finds a koala tunnel! The koala can then walk safely through a tunnel that leads into another section of its habitat.

While still in Australia, Jeff also encountered his favorite animals—snakes. In fact, he found himself removing a deadly snake from a woman's bathroom. That's right—her bathroom! Australia is home to some of the world's most venomous snakes. In Adelaide, Australia, Jeff met up with a man whose job it is to remove these snakes from people's homes. Snakes end up in private homes there more often than one might think! That's because the city was built on and around snake habitats. So sometimes these creatures slither into places where they aren't welcome!

Jeff and the snake-removal expert arrived at a home in which an eastern brown snake had taken up residence. Eastern brown snakes can be up to seven feet long and produce a highly toxic neurovenom. Needless to say, the homeowner did not want this new roommate! When the snake entered the bathroom, the homeowner shut the door, trapping it inside. Then she called the snake guys to come to her rescue! The snake was carefully removed using a special tool called a snake stick and dropped into a bag. Then it was rereleased into its natural habitat.

Filming of *The Jeff Corwin Experience* also brought Jeff to the Rufiji River in Africa. Jeff was riding down the river in a boat one day, enjoying the area's wildlife and scenery, when he came upon a big problem. Well, about fifty big problems, actually. Surrounding the boat in the waters of the river were fifty gigantic hippopotamuses!

Hippos are the third-largest land mammal on

Earth. They are three times the size of a small car, and they are known as one of the most aggressive animals in the world. Many consider them to be the most dangerous animal in all of Africa. Even crocodiles are afraid of them! So Jeff knew they had to exercise caution. The crew slowed their boat and cut its engine so as to not disturb the hippos. It was tense for a few minutes, but Jeff and his crew eventually drifted past the hippos.

Jeff certainly had a good time creating *The Jeff Corwin Experience*, but it was also a lot of long hours and hard work. To create one forty-eight-minute episode required about two weeks of traveling and shooting. It was also a serious job. *The Jeff Corwin Experience* explored and taught viewers about important issues, such as endangered species, sustainability, and global warming.

These were issues that are very meaningful to Jeff, and he had an idea to bring his knowledge of conservation and wildlife closer to home. In 2000, while still working on *Going Wild with Jeff Corwin*, Jeff approached the South Shore Natural Science Center with his next big idea: he wanted to create an environmental exhibit that would represent the ecosystems of southeastern Massachusetts. He would also help them raise the funds to build it.

The South Shore Natural Science Center has always been near and dear to Jeff's heart, as he spent nearly every afternoon there from ages nine to sixteen. He knew it was a place that showed people the connection between humans and their local environment. Jeff wanted people to recognize that the south shore of Massachusetts is home to an extraordinary natural habitat. Jeff worries that people often overlook the wildlife in their own backyard, and he feels it should be celebrated.

Jeff decided to call his creation EcoZone. EcoZone opened its doors in 2002 and is a hands-on, interactive learning exhibit area. Jeff did not want anything in EcoZone to be off limits or behind glass. The more people interact with the exhibits at EcoZone, the more they get out of it. The exhibit contains quaking bogs, estuaries, ponds, and swamps. Within the habitats, visitors can experience everything from a life-size model of a maple tree to a hollowed-out log large enough to crawl through to frogs and turtles in ponds. To date, being involved with EcoZone is still one of Jeff's proudest career achievements. He loves seeing kids—and people of all ages–having fun learning about Massachusetts habitats, and knowing that he was a part of that.

The following year turned out to be a big one for Jeff. In 2003, Jeff completed his graduate studies work. He finally held a master of science degree in Wildlife and Fisheries Conservation from the University of Massachusetts Amherst. And while that was a milestone in Jeff's life, it didn't outshine the fact that 2003 also was the year his first daughter, Maya Rose, was born. Jeff says that being a father has made his feelings about conservation even stronger. He feels that even if we don't want to protect our environment out of a sense of responsibility, we should do it for the next generation.

Jeff says, "What a kick in the pants to produce children that will inherit an unhealthy world. We spend all this time investing in medicine, health care, and clothing. But the most important thing we can do for them is give them a healthy planet. My love for nature comes from my love for animals, my fascination for the natural world, and my concern for the future of our natural heritage. But now I'm a conservationist because I have children. I am biologically contributing to the next generation. I have an obligation to ensure that they have the resources that I have had."

But, sadly, Jeff feels as though our generation has had moments of failure that cannot be corrected. Since Maya was born, there are species of animals that have become extinct. Maya will never have an opportunity to know them or see them firsthand.

After becoming a father, Jeff learned how hard it can be to make time for both his work life and his family life. He loves being a father; it is the most important job he has. But at the same time, he knows he has to take advantage of opportunities that build his career and keep him in the eyes of the public. And that means he has to travel and be away from his family quite often.

Jeff travels as much as ten months each year, and he finds it hard to be away from his family. While it's not possible to take them on most of his trips, Jeff does sometimes bring his family on the road. Maya has been to Central America, Africa, and throughout the United States—all before the age of five. Jeff remembers, "Maya spent her first birthday with a picnic lunch and a giraffe at a wildlife center in South Africa." That's one well-traveled little girl! Jeff continues, "The payoff of all the hard work is that my family gets to experience things others do not, and develop an appreciation for this great planet that we live on."

To round out Jeff's amazing year, 2003 was also when Jeff took his interest in teaching people about nature and conservation to another level. Jeff wrote his first book, *Living on the Edge: Amazing Relationships in the Natural World*. The title of the book refers to the idea that wildlife lives on the edge, just like Jeff does!

Since the age of twelve, it's been Jeff's dream to write a book. In an interview about the book, Jeff said, "I always dreamed of two things: hosting an animal show on TV and writing a book. Now I can say I've done both." Jeff is very proud of his first book. He poured his heart into it, and even took most of the photographs that appear in it.

In all of Jeff's work, whether it be books, television, or public speaking, he tries to teach one important message: we are all responsible for sustainable using, or saving Earth's natural resources. If we don't do it, the next generation will have to pay the price! Jeff feels that our worth as people can be measured by how we treat our planet. That's why Jeff stresses the importance of using Earth's resources in a way that will allow future generations to use them, too. We should aim to pass on a planet that is as biodiverse, healthy, biologically rich, and ecologically stable as it is now. And we should try to make it even more so!

To further this cause, Jeff joined the board of directors of Defenders of Wildlife in 2004. Defenders of Wildlife is a national, nonprofit organization that protects America's native animals and plants by educating people and helping them act on behalf of nature. Defenders of Wildlife has a hands-on, real-world, and practical approach to protecting resources. They work with lawmakers and the government to help create laws that protect animals. Jeff is impressed by their original solutions to conservation challenges. He is honored to be a part of such a great organization.

While Jeff certainly had a lot on his plate, he was still hungry for more! So, in June 2005, Jeff signed on to create another Animal Planet program, called

Corwin's Quest. The series was filmed over many months on five continents and focuses on a theme for each episode, such as "sound" or "extremes," rather than the location. *Corwin's Quest* brings viewers face-to-face with blue whales, reticulated pythons, vervet monkeys, Mexican free-tailed bats, desert scorpions, killer snails, and everything in between. And, as usual, Jeff had a wild time with his animal costars.

While filming one episode of *Corwin's Quest*, Jeff found himself swimming with great white sharks off the coast of South Africa. Great whites are the largest meat-eating shark in the ocean. They can reach more than twenty feet in length. They have enormous, razor-sharp teeth—sometimes up to three thousand of them at a time! Great whites are predators at the top of the marine ecosystem, making them important to the health of oceans. They generally hunt marine mammals such as sea lions, seals, and dolphins.

Jeff was cage diving to study the sharks. That means he was lowered into the ocean inside a protective steel cage. From inside the safety of the cage, Jeff could film and study the sharks.

In order to be able to breathe while he was under water, Jeff was wearing a heavy dome-shaped metal helmet that had oxygen pumped into it through a tube. It was so heavy that it took two people to put it on. If something went wrong, it wasn't possible for him to get it off by himself.

Suddenly, the fresh oxygen wasn't replacing the carbon dioxide Jeff was breathing out fast enough. Jeff began to sweat and feel uncomfortable. He started to panic, and signaled the other divers and crew for help. But nobody seemed to see him! So in order to save himself, Jeff squirmed out of the shark cage. He swam toward the surface of the water and was about to be pulled back onto the boat. And that was precisely the moment when a sixteen-foot great white shark swam up behind Jeff.

The shark circled within only a few feet of Jeff, who was still bobbing around in the ocean. Great whites, or any other type of shark, rarely attack human beings. Jeff's crew remained calm and dragged Jeff back into the boat. It wasn't until after Jeff was safe that the crew informed him that he had gone swimming with a great white shark!

For another episode of *Corwin's Quest*, Jeff jumped off one of the world's highest bridges. That's right, Jeff jumped off a bridge! But he didn't do it just the one time. Jeff plunged from a six-hundred-foot bridge in Italy *ten* times! He was attached to a bungee cord, of course, and had a 16-mm video camera attached to his chest. And he did it all in the name of science.

The goal was to compare the speed of Jeff's fall against that of a trained falcon. But the bird didn't cooperate the first time, so Jeff had to keep bungee jumping until he got the shot he needed. For each bungee jump, Jeff stood on the rail of the bridge staring down at the rocks below. That's right—there were rocks, not water, below him! Whenever the falcon trainer was ready to release the bird, Jeff was told to jump. Jeff said it was very scary to jump off something so high.

After each jump, Jeff hung upside down four hundred feet in the air until he was lifted back up again. He says, "My back was killing me." It got to the point that Jeff was in too much pain to continue doing more takes. So a member of the crew was chosen to be Jeff's stunt double for the last few jumps. Normally, Jeff does his own stunts, but this time, he was relieved to have a stand-in!

In another episode, the show was being filmed in Uganda, Africa. Jeff and his crew found themselves in the middle of what is known as a chimp hunt. A chimp hunt is a phenomenon in which a group of about twenty to thirty chimpanzees organizes to attack simultaneously another group of smaller animals. It is a group hunting behavior rarely caught on film.

In this case, Jeff and his crew watched as chimps moved in toward a group of about fifty colobus monkeys in the treetops. Some of the larger chimps climbed into the trees, moving up to the branches where the colobus were. Other chimps stayed on the ground to capture any colobus monkeys that might fall or try to escape by way of the ground.

The colobus leaped from branch to branch, tree to tree, and even over a two-hundred-foot ravine to try to escape. It was a matter of life and death for the medium- to large-size monkeys, so they would do anything to survive the attack. But it was also a matter of life and death for the chimps, too, who needed to eat. Jeff didn't know which animal to root for! In the end, the chimps captured a few of their prey, and rejoiced in their meal. Jeff felt proud of the chimps for the capture, but also felt awful for the poor colobus victims. Nonetheless, it was marvelous for him to witness.

On another trip to Africa for *Corwin's Quest*, Jeff was in the mountains of Uganda searching for gorillas. He had been feeling ill during the entire trip, and had lost a lot of weight. He eventually came to realize that he was very sick with malaria and African tick fever, *at the same time*! It was a taxing trip for Jeff's health, certainly. But he pushed through, taking off only one day from filming. And in the end, it paid off! After days of endless trekking, Jeff found himself sitting just a few feet away from an entire troop of gorillas, including the amazing giant silverback gorilla!

It was also for *Corwin's Quest* that Jeff had his teeth cleaned by a live shrimp! Jeff wanted to show viewers how cool cleaner shrimp are. Cleaner shrimp are very valuable to the coral reef community. They survive on tiny, parasitic crustaceans and dead skin. These things often build up on fish, so cleaner shrimp remove them. The cleaner shrimp have a meal and the fish can swim free of irritation—everybody wins! Several cleaner shrimp will clean a single fish at a time. They dash around over the fish's body, munching away the parasites.

To show how this process works, Jeff ate a large meal, and was sure to leave bits of food in his teeth.

Then he went scuba diving in the ocean near the Great Barrier Reef, off the coast of Australia. Jeff found a cleaner shrimp and put it to work. He put the live shrimp in his mouth, and the cleaner shrimp proceeded to eat the food remains from Jeff's teeth!

For the next several years, Jeff's career continued to thrive. He was experiencing tremendous success in all areas of his life, and having a great time doing it. But he wanted to do a project that reached a new audience. That's why he approached the news network CNN with the idea for a new TV series called *Planet in Peril*.

Jeff's idea was to show people how environmental conditions are interconnected: climate change, habitat loss, pollution, and human population growth. Each of these problems affects the next. In an interview with *UMass Magazine Online*, Jeff once explained, "Everything is knotted together to make one great living fabric."

CNN really liked the idea, so they agreed to make the show. Jeff had appeared on CNN many times as an animal expert, so it was rewarding for him to present them with an idea, then see it come to fruition.

In 2007, *Planet in Peril* aired as a four-hour documentary that examined our changing planet. It also featured correspondents Anderson Cooper and Dr. Sanjay Gupta. To create the series, Jeff traveled the globe, from the Brazilian rain forest to the arctic tundra. He was greatly affected by what he saw during filming. For example, when Jeff was in Southeast Asia, he walked into silent rain forests. They were silent because every bird, lizard, and mammal was gone, and had likely died.

During his time in Madagascar, an island off the coast of Africa, Jeff found himself feeling bittersweet. He realized that he could potentially discover a new species there. But at the same time, anything he discovered would probably not survive long because its habitat was being completely destroyed by humans.

Jeff also traveled to the North Pole to study polar bears for the series. He had the chance to work side by side with one of the world's best biologists, tracking and observing the bears. Polar bears are one of nature's most powerful predators, but Jeff says, "Their future is uncertain due to climate change."

Jeff recalls staring out onto an abyss of ice, being awestruck by nature's power, and how cold it was! He says the temperatures were around 60 degrees below freezing, and that every time he had a runny nose from the cold, there was an instant icicle hanging from the tip of his nose!

It was during the filming of *Planet in Peril* that Jeff had one of his most frightening animal experiences. An Asian elephant attacked him. The incident happened on March 22, 2007, in the country of Cambodia, in Southeast Asia.

Jeff was reporting on Cambodia's wild elephant population. As little as one hundred years ago, there were thousands of Asian elephants in the rain forests of Southeast Asia. But today, Asian elephants are nearly extinct in the wild. There are only about thirty thousand of them left. This is because humans are tearing down the forests in which they live, and because humans kill elephants for their tusks.

Jeff was at a wildlife rehabilitation center, where he was helping workers handle three of the elephants. Twice a day, every day, the elephants were taken to a lagoon to be washed and exercised. Jeff was talking to Anderson Cooper and turned his back on one of the elephants. Elephants are complicated animals that experience emotions, such as happiness, anger, and jealousy. When Jeff turned away, the pachyderm decided to let Jeff know he didn't want to be ignored.

Suddenly, the enormous elephant was right over Jeff's shoulder. Before Jeff could react, the elephant grabbed Jeff's arm in his mouth and thrashed Jeff back and forth several times. Asian elephants grow to be as much as twenty-one feet long, stand up to ten feet tall, and weigh up to eleven thousand pounds. They are thousands of times stronger than humans. In fact, the trunk of an elephant can lift a seven-hundred-pound tree limb. So in the creature's mouth, Jeff was nothing more than a rag doll.

When the elephant grabbed Jeff, he instantly crushed many of the muscles, ligaments, and tendons in Jeff's arm. Jeff screamed, and thought he might black out from the pain. Within seconds, the elephant handlers stepped in. They got the elephant to release Jeff from its jaws. If the handlers had not reacted as quickly as they did, Jeff probably would have died.

The entire incident was caught on film, as CNN cameras were rolling at the moment the elephant attacked. And in spite of the pain Jeff was in, he continued reporting the story! In an interview after the incident, Jeff said, "I was there to investigate the conflict between elephants and humans. You don't get a better example of the story than what had just happened to me."

In the end, Jeff healed fairly well. He felt lucky to be alive, and was reminded just how powerful animals can be.

Of all the animals in the world, it's only the human variety that Jeff fears. Jeff believes people are far more unpredictable, dangerous, and destructive than any other animal. He has been in small planes that nearly crashed or had emergency landings. He's witnessed coups d'état and revolutions, and had his hotel set on fire. And he'd still prefer a cobra that's a little peeved to any of them.

No matter what kind of journey Jeff is on, or where in the world he is, he always exercises extreme caution. While he does want to create a unique experience for his viewers, he would never do anything to jeopardize the wildlife or himself. Jeff has a family that loves him and needs him to return from his adventures in one piece. Even Jeff's wife, Natasha, doesn't worry *too* much about her husband: "Jeff is a big boy and he's a smart man. He has the utmost respect for wildlife."

Jeff is also responsible for keeping his TV crew safe from harm. That's why he and his staff do a great deal of research on the region and its wildlife before going into the field. And if Jeff senses that something could be dangerous, he simply won't do it. While Jeff treasures his wild times, safety always comes first.

CHAPTER FIVE

Traveling Man

After Jeff completed *Planet in Peril*, he wanted to turn his focus on his own country—the United States. He approached the Travel Channel with an idea for a new series about travel in the United States. Jeff wanted to use the medium of television to explore his homeland. Jeff is best known for his work with animals, but the new TV series gave Jeff the opportunity to explore another of his passions—adventure travel.

The first program in the series is called *Into Alaska with Jeff Corwin*. *Into Alaska* is an eight-part series in which he investigates the amazing natural wonders of Alaska. The show was tremendously successful, thanks to Jeff's pioneer spirit! He did everything from working on a commercial crab boat to scaling parts of Mount McKinley. Mount McKinley is the coldest mountain on Earth. It is so tall that it creates its own weather! Nonetheless, Jeff decided to climb it. He battled slippery ice, blinding light, and thin air as he ascended. But the amazing view at the top made it well worth it!

While in Alaska, Jeff also explored Ruth Glacier, where it can feel as cold as 148 degrees below zero! Glaciers are essentially enormous mounds of ice that are constantly moving, flowing, and shifting in the ocean. From the snowy surface, they appear solid, but underneath, huge crevasses can form, which present danger. So Jeff and his crew had to be especially careful when hiking the glacier. These crevices can be hundreds of feet deep, and become blue in their deepest parts. To get a better look at one, Jeff was lowered down into a crevice. He was suspended several feet below the surface and just hung there above an icy abyss until being lifted up again.

Into Alaska with Jeff Corwin gave Jeff a chance to get friendly with Alaska's animals, too. Jeff guided a team of sled dogs across the Goddard Glacier and kayaked with humpback whales. He even had a fishing competition with brown bears! One day, while fishing in the Margot River, Jeff noticed that there was a brown bear fishing just down the river from him. Brown bears are America's largest land predator. These monstrous creatures can weigh up to fifteen hundred pounds. To get that large, brown bears in Alaska feed on live fish in Alaska's icy-cold waters. They have to feed heavily during the summer in order to fatten up for winter, when they hibernate for up to eight months.

As Jeff caught fish, he noticed that the bear down the river was also catching fish. Jeff was equipped with a tool—a fishing pole—and could certainly outfish a bear, which just had its mouth and paws to rely on. Or so he thought! So Jeff spent the afternoon trying to catch more fish than the bear. It was a fishing competition! In the end, Jeff's manmade fishing tool couldn't beat out the bear's natural tools, or its hunger-driven determination!

Jeff spent nearly a year filming in Alaska. He says, "I had a rich, complete, fulfilling experience working on that show." Travel Channel viewers loved *Into*

Alaska with Jeff Corwin so much that it was followed up with a second show called *Into America's West*. Jeff explored the length and breadth of the West Coast, from the Canadian Rockies to New Mexico, all the while on the lookout for America's wildlife, like mountain lions, bobcats, and black bears, to name only a few. For *Into America's West*, Jeff did everything from working on a cattle ranch delivering calves to following the trails of Lewis and Clark.

For the show, Jeff investigated the Grand Canyon, Mount Baker, the plains of Montana, and Yellowstone National Park, learning how some of these incredible places were formed, and how they are still changing.

Jeff found the *Into* series enjoyable to create, not only because of the adventures, but because he feels that Americans forget that there is still an incredible frontier in their own backyards. He wants Americans to feel excited about the rich diversity of their own country. Jeff hopes to do another program for the series, perhaps *Into the East*.

And Jeff Corwin certainly is not slowing down. Jeff has been working on numerous projects, including a documentary on polar bears in the Arctic. He has also created another documentary called *The Vanishing Frog*, which aired on Animal Planet in late 2008.

In *The Vanishing Frog*, Jeff investigates the massive and somewhat sudden extinction of amphibians around the world. Amphibians are becoming extinct at a rate matched only by how quickly the dinosaurs were wiped out. Two hundred species of frogs and other amphibians have become extinct in the last decade. Jeff predicts that in the next three decades, the situation will become even worse: we'll lose 50 percent more of those that remain.

Amphibians are important to predator-prey relationships, agriculture, and science. But amphibians are also an indicator of environmental quality, water quality, and temperature. When amphibian species are suffering, it is an early warning sign that something is wrong within an ecosystem. It could mean the other wildlife in the ecosystem will suffer as well. That is why Jeff feels it so very important to investigate the problem of our vanishing frogs.

In addition to his upcoming television work, Jeff is also in the process of writing several new books.

His second book for adults, *100 Heartbeats*, explores a very scary ecological situation—the moment when there are fewer than one hundred life-forms left before extinction. He's been globetrotting to study the final moments of failure or success for particular species. Jeff is also in the process of creating a series of kids' books about nature. The series is published by Penguin Young Readers Group and combines nonfiction and fiction books—including this biography, a fascinating book about U.S. ecosystems, and a fun, fictional Junior Explorer series. These books come from Jeff's heart because he is the father of two daughters. That's right! In 2008, Jeff and Natasha became the parents of another baby girl, named Marina. When Jeff looks at his children, he is constantly reminded of how important it is for humans to leave behind a planet that is biodiverse and healthy.

Jeff hopes that his books for kids will help children realize they have the power to change the world. Jeff says, "Sometimes I think that young people don't think they matter. But everyone leaves behind an ecological footprint. (An ecological footprint is a measure of how much of Earth's resources we each consume.) I think it's important that people recognize that—

realize that every day, you are going to do something that impacts the world. Do you want that impact to be positive or negative?"

Jeff wants kids to begin taking small steps toward saving Earth's resources. Remember: every step is a step in the right direction! You can begin doing this by just looking at your daily habits.

For example, think about the plastic water bottles from which we all drink. Drinking a bottle of water provides you with the liquid your body needs to survive. But at the same time, by drinking water out of a plastic bottle, you are using a container that will last for thousands of years. If you drink that water through a straw, you are using even more plastic that will remain on Earth far longer than you.

You can also try the Trash Challenge that Jeff often poses to kids when he gives speeches. Rather than throwing things away, save every single piece of trash you produce in a single day. That's every water bottle, every scrap of leftover food, every wrapper, every piece of product packaging, every piece of paper . . . you get the idea! Jeff says, "No toilet paper, please! But save everything else."

At the end of the day, you will probably be

shocked at your impact with regard to waste: In any given twenty-four-hour period, the average American creates about five pounds of trash! As Jeff says, "If you think you don't have an impact, just look at your garbage. Think about how much energy it took to create it, and where it will all end up." Jeff says that simple examples like these can make kids realize firsthand how much of an effect they have on Earth's health.

Jeff's kids' books also explore the idea that all of Earth's creatures play an important role in their own ecosystem. He worries that many people judge animals: they think some are better, more important, or more valuable to the world than others. "I don't look at animals as one being nice and one being bad—the pretty feathers of a bird as opposed to the fangs of a rattlesnake," Jeff says. In Jeff's mind, all animals are created equal! Jeff adds, "It's important to understand that no one creature is greater than another. All species are significant and have earned a place at the table of life."

To see this in your everyday life, Jeff urges kids to look in their very own yards and communities. You might find a frog in a stream, a bald eagle in a tree, a mountain lion, a bear, or a box turtle. It's easy for everyone to recognize the importance of saving tigers or monkeys. But in your community, it's unlikely that it is a tiger that needs saving. Instead, it could be a local animal species or a particular habitat. There are examples of wildlife failures everywhere. But there can also be examples of success! And that part is up to us.

Jeff wants others to know that for many threatened species and habitats, we are nearly at the point of no return—but we aren't there yet. He says, "While we live in what could end up being the dark days of conservation, we also live in a time of incredible hope." We can still save what remains.

So what if you want to go even further than taking small steps? What if you want to help Earth in the same ways that Jeff has? Well, you can follow in his footsteps! Start by going to the sources: books, magazines, and Web sites are great resources of information. Jeff says, "Read up on areas and animals that interest you."

Even better, interact with other people who share an interest in nature! Sign up for classes, attend nature camps, or volunteer at a local science center or preserve. And, of course, try your best to do well in school. School would have been easier for Jeff if he had been able to study hard and get better grades. Jeff reminds kids, "Your formal education is crucial. These things will help you hone in on an area of naturalism that most appeals to you. The most important thing is to be active and involved."

Jeff firmly believes that if kids work hard and trust in themselves, there is very little they cannot achieve. There may be obstacles to achieving your dreams—there were for him! "Many people in my life thought my goals were impossible or silly and that they wouldn't materialize. But I didn't believe them," Jeff says. He learned that the people who really succeed are those who are persistent. He offers, "If there isn't a path carved out for you, blaze a new trail. Carve your *own* path; find alternative ways to get there. Always believe in yourself because no one else will. Retain personal passion, drive, and the confidence that you can do it."

CHAPTER SIX

Where Everybody Knows Your Name

Jeff Corwin's fans know him as the funny, charming face of animal conservation. But who is Jeff when the cameras have shut off? Jeff wears many hats in his life: he is a husband, a father, a runner, a chef . . . you name it! Let's take a look inside what it's like being Jeff Corwin!

When it comes to life experiences, Jeff Corwin has seen and done a lot! Take his television appearances for example. Not only does Jeff have his own shows, but he has been featured on *Iron Chef America, The*

Oprah Winfrey Show, The Tonight Show with Jay Leno, Today, Good Morning America, The Early Show, Access Hollywood, and *Extra.* He even made a cameo appearance on an episode of the hit crime show *CSI: Miami,* in which he helped detectives retrieve a human foot from inside a live crocodile. Jeff won an Emmy for Best Performer in a Children's Series, and *Men's Journal* once called him "the world's greatest animal show host." Jeff appeared in *Maxim*'s fall fashion issue and on *Entertainment Weekly*'s highly regarded It List.

And then there're the places he's been! Jeff says, "I've been around the world probably five or six times. There are countries that few people go to, like Borneo, that I've been to many times. I go to Africa probably three or four times a year. But there are still a few places out there that I'm longing to go . . . like Antarctica and mainland China, especially to see the giant Chinese salamander."

Despite Jeff's fame and incredible achievements, he still feels he is a humble guy. And his family helps him stay that way. As Jeff's wife, Natasha, said when *People* magazine named him one of the Most Beautiful People, "Okay, Mr. Beautiful, take out the trash." Jeff's family is proud of him, of course. But it's not because of his success on television. They just appreciate that Jeff is a good son, husband, and father. He says, "I don't live in a TV world. I live a regular life. I don't live around a lot of animals. . . . I live five miles from where I grew up." To Jeff, fame is just a moment in his life—it's fleeting. And that's okay, because he knows that, at heart, he will always be a conservationist and naturalist.

Jeff realizes the blessings in his life: "My career has a value. It is a tool to allow me to share the message I want to share, and to build a life for my family that I want them to have. But that's all it is, and life outside of that with friends and family is far more significant."

Downtime is rare in Jeff's life. He's usually traveling from continent to continent. But when Jeff is at home, he's at his house—a hundred-year-old farmhouse set on a twenty-two-acre island. The island sits a mile off the coast of Boston's south shore and is shared by twelve other families. But only five families, including Jeff's, live there year-round. It can be reached only by water or on foot after the tide has gone out. It contains woods, marshland, and a fruitful animal habitat—all of Jeff's favorite things.

Jeff shares his home with his wife, Natasha, and daughters, Maya and Marina. When Jeff thinks about his home and family, he says, "If there is a heaven, I hope it will be something like this." And the only pets the Corwins have are two cats. "I don't have any exotics living around me. My personal philosophy, after a lifetime of working and living with animals, is that exotic, nontraditional animals should only be kept for acceptable purposes, such as wildlife rehabilitation, outreach education, and conservation programs. But I do love animals, and I love being around them," he says.

Jeff's parents still live in the house in Norwell where Jeff was raised, which is one of the reasons he still lives in the area. He also just can't imagine living anywhere else! Jeff says, "I have always loved the seasons, culture, architecture, sense of community, food, coastline, and history of New England."

Jeff admits that when he was younger, he was very driven, and didn't stop to enjoy his success as much as he should have. "But now I don't feel the pressure to plow on through and not smell the roses," he says. And smell the roses he does!

When Jeff is home, he enjoys many hobbies, like hunting for beach glass and foraging for mushrooms with his daughter Maya. Jeff also likes to go antiquing with Natasha, fish, and practice photography.

Jeff also loves cooking for his friends and family when he has the time. He tries to cook and eat locally grown foods, like the blueberries, apples, and raspberries he grows on his own property and the lobsters, clams, and mussels he catches from the waters around his house. He says that people should know where their food comes from and how far it had to travel in order to get to our tables. It's one small way that we can save Earth's resources.

When Jeff is home, he also spends time with friends, hanging out on the beach by a fire or enjoying a meal together. Jeff and Natasha's friends are teachers, artists, businesspeople, and more. Some of Jeff's friends are people he has known since he was a kid in Norwell, and others are people he's met more recently.

One of Jeff's great passions in life, aside from animals and family, is running. He runs about forty miles a week. But he never, ever runs to music. In a

Runner's World article, Jeff explained, "The last time I listened to music, I almost got hit by an airplane. I was jogging on a jungle runway in the middle of Belize and I kept feeling this weird wind every ten minutes that would blow by me." It turns out that "wind" was actually a plane trying to land! But the music in Jeff's ears was so loud, he could not hear the plane or the local villagers telling him to move! Needless to say, Jeff survived. But the plane's pilot was very upset with him!

So what does the future hold for everyone's favorite animal enthusiast? Jeff wants to continue to grow in his career, whether that's through books, different types of shows, or different types of audiences. At the end of his life, Jeff would like to be remembered as a naturalist and not just as an entertainer. He, of course, enjoys the entertainment element of his shows. But he feels that teaching people about endangered species and the environment is more important.

Though Jeff has no immediate plans to stop doing television shows, he envisions a calmer life for himself in the future. Jeff once said, "I see myself as a quirky science professor at a New England college. But I refuse to be boring! I'll be the teacher who makes you laugh." There would be no shortage of students signing up for *that* class!

Wherever the future endeavors of Jeff Corwin will lead him remains to be seen. But one thing is certain—it's sure to be a wild time!

Resources

Defenders of Wildlife:
www.defenders.org
Events near you: http://www.defenders.org/take_action/upcom
ing_events/index.php

JASON Project:
www.jason.org
Rescue your local ecosystem and protect diverse species from
extinction. Register for JASON: http://www.jason.org/Public/Get
Involved/GetInvolved.aspx?pos=7

New England Wildlife Center:
www.newildlife.com

United Nations Environmental Programme:
www.unep.org

World Wildlife Fund (WWF):
www.worldwildlife.org
Learn about the five different ways you can get involved with the
WWF, including adopting an animal and learning to live green:
http://www.worldwildlife.org/how/index.html

Bibliography

Personal interview

Conducted on August 2–3, 2008

Books

Living on the Edge: Amazing Relationships in the Natural World
by Jeff Corwin
Rodale, 2003

Norwell
Images of America series
by James Pierotti, with a foreword by Jeff Corwin
Arcadia Publishing, 2006

Articles

Boston Globe Archives:
"Celebrity Brings Environment Home"
by Kimberly Atkins, *Globe* staff correspondent
January 13, 2002, page 3, Globe South

"A TV Host's Exotic Experiences Never End"
by Teri Borseti, *Globe* correspondent
December 18, 2003, page H2, Life at Home

Web Sites/Web Articles

Boston Globe:
"After 20 years, Corwin still thrives on call of the wild"
by Robert Carroll, *Globe* staff
January 4, 2004
http://www.boston.com/news/science/articles/2004/01/04/after_20_
years_corwin_still_thrives_on_call_of_the_wild/

"Hanging with . . . Jeff Corwin: The South Shore–bred Animal
Planet host goes fishing on a sunny Sunday afternoon"
September 1, 2006
http://www.boston.com/ae/events/articles/2006/09/01/hanging_
with__jeff_corwin/

"He's just crackers about animals: Jeff Corwin cuts vacation short to
bring his critters to Plymouth"
by Robert Carroll, *Globe* correspondent
May 11, 2006
http://www.boston.com/news/local/massachusetts/articles/2006/05/
11/hes_just_crackers_about_animals/

"Where the wild things are: Jeff Corwin finds creature comforts at
home, abroad"
by Bella English, *Globe* staff
September 18, 2007
http://www.boston.com/yourlife/articles/2007/09/18/where_the_
wild_things_are/?page=2

Defenders Magazine:
"Defenders in Action: Five Questions for Jeff Corwin"
Summer 2005
http://www.defenders.org/newsroom/defenders_magazine/
summer_2005/defenders_in_action_five_questions_for_jeff_corwin
.php?ht=

CNN transcript:
Larry King Live
"Interview with Jeff Corwin"
July 26, 2005
http://transcripts.cnn.com/TRANSCRIPTS/0507/26/lkl.01.html

CNN transcript:
"Live From . . . Interview with Jeff Corwin"
November 10, 2003
http://transcripts.cnn.com/TRANSCRIPTS/0311/10/lol.11.html

Defenders of Wildlife:
http://www.defenders.org

Entertainment Weekly:
"Jeff Corwin's 5-Year Plan"
by Karyn L. Barr
http://www.ew.com/ew/article/0,,535733,00.html

Extreme Science:
http://www.extremescience.com

Frog Matters:
"Where in the world was Jeff Corwin (in early April)?"
The Frog Blog of Jeff Davis
May 7, 2008
http://frogmatters.wordpress.com/2008/05/07/where-in-the-world-was-jeff-corwin-in-early-april/

Heartland USA Magazine:
http://www.heartlandusamagazine.com/lifestyles/life_corwin.php

Hollywood.com:
"Jeff Corwin unveils a 'Planet in Peril'"
by Emily Christianson
http://www.hollywood.com/feature/Planet_in_Peril_Jeff_Corwin_Anderson_Cooper/4954710

JASON Project:
www.jason.org

Live discussion with Jeff Corwin on Animal Planet's Web site:
http://animal.discovery.com/fansites/jeffcorwin/chat/transcript.html

Merriam Webster Dictionary Online:
http://www.merriam-webster.com

MLive.com:
Everything Michigan
"Wild time coming to Whiting: Animal Planet host, Jeff Corwin, to
thrill, educate with 'Tales from the Field'"
by Carol Azizian (*Flint Journal*)
May 1, 2008
http://www.mlive.com/flintjournal/entertainment/index
.ssf/2008/05/wild_time_coming_to_whiting_an.html

MSN Encarta Encyclopedia Online:
http://www.msnencarta.com

MSNBC:
"Jeff Corwin continues monkey business: Kooky biologist's latest
show is 'Corwin's Quest'"
Fri., June 24, 2005 (updated 11:53 a.m. ET)
http://www.msnbc.msn.com/id/8293179/

New York Magazine:
"What Animal Scares Jeff Corwin the Most?"
July 20, 2007
http://nymag.com/daily/intel/2007/07/what_animal_scares_jeff_
corwin.html

Notable Biographies:
http://www.notablebiographies.com/newsmakers2/2005-A-Fi/
Corwin-Jeff.html

People magazine:
"Jeff Corwin: Animal Show Host"
May 13, 2002
http://www.people.com/people/archive/article/0,,20137016,00.html

Runner's World:
"I'm a runner: Jeff Corwin"
by Ben Court
August 2004
http://www.newrunner.com/article/0,7120,s6-243-410--9274-0,00
.html

South Shore Natural Science Center:
http://www.ssnsc.org/ecozone.htm

The New Hampshire (The Student Publication of the University of
New Hampshire):
"Jeff Corwin shares his animal adventures"
by Cara Murphy
December 3, 2004
http://media.www.tnhonline.com/media/storage/paper674/
news/2004/12/03/ArtsLiving/Jeff-Corwin.Shares.His.Animal
.Adventures-820438.shtml

Tripod.com:
"A Chat with Jeff Corwin"
http://members.tripod.com/~Poet70/Jeffchat.html

UMass Magazine Online:
"Experiencing Jeff Corwin: I can't think of a creature that doesn't
fascinate me"
by Christopher O'Carroll
Fall 2003
http://umassmag.com/fall_2003/Experiencing_Jeff_Corwin_569.
html

United Nations Environmental Programme:
www.unep.org

USA Today:
"CNN takes stock of a 'Planet in Peril'"
by Frazier Moore, AP television writer
October 22, 2007
http://usatoday.com/life/television/news/2007-10-21-cnn_N.htm

Washington Post transcript:
"Animal Week: Animal Planet's Jeff Corwin"
http://www.washingtonpost.com/wp-dyn/content/discussion/2006
/04/06/DI2006040601068.html

World Wildlife Fund:
www.worldwildlife.org